The
Spelling Bee

by Stephanie Wilder

illustrated by Nicole Wong

PEARSON

Scott
Foresman

Editorial Offices: Glenview, Illinois • Parsippany, New Jersey • New York, New York
Sales Offices: Needham, Massachusetts • Duluth, Georgia • Glenview, Illinois
Coppell, Texas • Ontario, California • Mesa, Arizona

Kate had a reputation for being a chatterbox. Each day her teacher, Mr. Harper, would be forced to say, "Kate, could you please stop whispering with Jess? You need to be paying attention!"

Jess was a pretty girl with long pigtails. She sat directly behind Kate in Mr. Harper's class. In the morning they often discussed what they would eat for lunch in the school cafeteria. Jess liked ham-and-cheese sandwiches. Kate favored bagels with cream cheese.

After lunch the conversation usually included their after-school plans. Today, though, the most important topic was the school-wide spring spelling bee, which would take place that evening in the school auditorium.

Kate felt nervous about standing in front of an audience. The entire school would be at the spelling bee, along with all the relatives of her classmates.

Although Kate was nervous, the possibility that she could be the fifth-grade winner excited her. She needed to share her feelings with Jess. Kate knew that Jess would understand since she, too, was nervous and excited.

As usual Mr. Harper was not pleased with their chatter.

"Quiet down, everyone," he said. "It is essential that we finish this work."

Kate faced forward in her chair and tried to concentrate on the afternoon grammar lesson. Despite her efforts, she kept becoming distracted by what lay ahead that night. Kate could think of nothing other than the spelling bee!

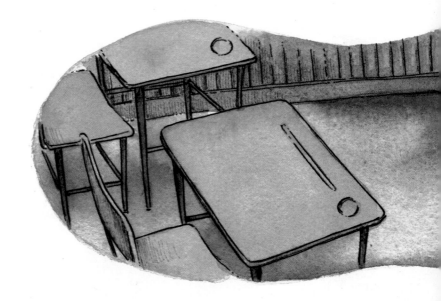

The minutes dragged by. Finally, Mr. Harper reviewed the homework assignment. The dismissal bell rang shortly after. Kate gathered her books.

"Kate," said Mr. Harper. "Please see me at my desk."

Kate approached her teacher. Yesterday Mr. Harper had said that he would have to see her after school if she kept making distractions. Kate feared that Mr. Harper might not let her participate in the spelling bee because of her constant disruptions.

"Kate," said Mr. Harper sternly. "I warned you yesterday not to disrupt the class again."

Kate wanted to cry. "Mr. Harper, I'm so sorry. I promise I won't ever talk during class again."

"That's what you said yesterday," said Mr. Harper.

"But, Mr. Harper," Kate pleaded, "tonight is the spelling bee. More than anything in the world, I want to be there!"

Mr. Harper looked puzzled. "Who said anything about missing the spelling bee? I called you to my desk to remind you that whispering is unfair to everyone. It keeps students from learning as well as they might. Each student deserves the best opportunity to learn, Kate."

Mr. Harper smiled. "I also called you up to wish you good luck in the spelling bee. I'll be rooting for you and your classmates."

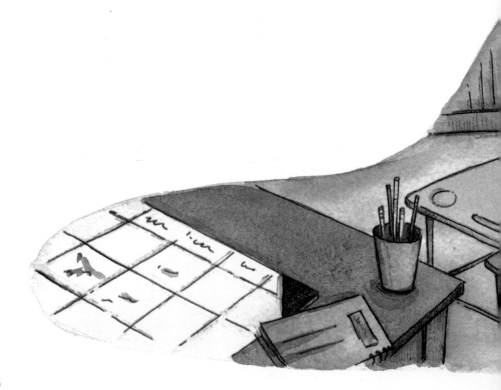

Kate was relieved that Mr. Harper was still letting her participate in the spelling bee. But she also knew that he was right about her chatting problem. "You've come a long way this year, Kate. Your expanded vocabulary will help you greatly in tonight's spelling bee," said Mr. Harper.

"Thanks Mr. Harper," said Kate.

Kate left the classroom, thinking of everything Mr. Harper had said. She couldn't wait for the spelling bee!

Kate hurried home. There were many things to do. She had to do her homework, eat dinner with her mom, and change into her lucky dress.

Kate's mom was waiting at home with some cookies and a glass of milk. Kate sat down to enjoy the treat. She talked with her mom about the big night that lay ahead.

"I'm so pleased, Kate," her mom said. "Nobody forced you to enter the spelling bee, but you took on the challenge anyway. You've worked so hard to improve your spelling and vocabulary. I know that you'll do well tonight!"

Kate grinned at her mom. She was proud of herself and the work she had done during the last year to improve her spelling and vocabulary. Her mind drifted back to a time when she hadn't felt happy about her learning.

Reading had always been difficult for Kate. It had become more frustrating with each passing year, as the amount of reading had increased in each grade.

Last spring, Kate was having serious difficulty in school. Her mom got together with Mrs. Miller, Kate's fourth-grade teacher, to find out why.

Both Mrs. Miller and Kate's mother knew that Kate was intelligent. They were sure that there was a good explanation for her struggles. Together they made an effort to discover the explanation and make some changes that would help Kate.

Kate's mom noticed that Kate was having a hard time getting her homework done. She also noticed that Kate seemed less happy about going to school with each passing day. Clearly something had to be done.

Kate's mom and Mrs. Miller decided that Kate should see Dr. Shaw, a counselor at her school. Dr. Shaw had Kate take some tests. Some of the tests were both fun and challenging. Others were challenging, but not at all fun. Finally Dr. Shaw finished, and Kate was able to go home.

A few weeks later, Kate's mom received a letter from the school about the tests that Kate had done with Dr. Shaw. They had shown that Kate had a learning disability called *dyslexia*.

At a meeting the next day, Dr. Shaw explained to Kate and her mom about dyslexia. He described how dyslexia was a reading disorder that caused the reader to see letters and symbols in the wrong order.

Kate was upset to find out she had this disorder. She felt frustrated that there was no medicine to cure it. Still, knowing that her reading problem had a name and that her teachers could help with it made Kate feel hopeful.

After Kate's dyslexia had been discovered, Mrs. Miller and Miss Zahn, the school's reading teacher, spent extra time with Kate for the rest of the school year. They taught her special methods that made reading less difficult.

The summer arrived. Kate's friends were going to camp, but she would be staying at home to practice her reading. Miss Zahn had given Kate a set of chapter books to read during the summer. Each book was accompanied by different activities. At first Kate wasn't interested in the books. The only thing she could think about was how much she missed her friends while they were at camp.

After a while, Kate realized that there were better things to do than feel sorry about being stuck at home. She thought of all the help her teachers had given her. If they believed her reading could improve, then so would she! Kate decided to get to work on her summer reading.

Kate set weekly goals for completing the chapter books and their activities. She taught her mom the new methods she'd learned. Sometimes they took turns reading chapters out loud together. Other times Kate read a few paragraphs silently before reading them out loud.

Kate and her mom would discuss each chapter as they read. They enjoyed working together. Kate now felt excited about her progress. In the past, Kate worshipped the summer as a break from school. But now she realized that the summer was also a great time for learning!

As a reward for all the hard work she did over the summer, Kate's mom made her pancakes on the first morning of fifth grade. Pancakes were Kate's favorite.

"Kate," her mom said, "you've worked incredibly hard to improve your reading skills. I know you're prepared for everything that fifth grade will throw at you. Hopefully you'll be able to maintain a perfect attendance record this year. You'll be reading many interesting and exciting books, and you won't want to miss a moment!"

Kate finished her pancakes. While getting dressed for school, she thought about Mr. Harper, her new teacher. Everyone said that he was very strict. Kate hoped that she would like him and that he would like her.

Kate left the house. Turning to her mom, she said, "I'm going to keep working hard at my reading and spelling. Maybe in the spring, I'll enter the spelling bee!"

Kate's mom was happy to see her daughter excited about school. She knew that Kate would be guaranteed a successful year in fifth grade if she didn't give up on herself and her studies.

The school year began. Reading and spelling were still hard for Kate, but the special methods she had learned were a big help to her. With extra effort and some help from her teacher and her mom, she was able to do well.

Mr. Harper was strict indeed. However, as Kate became acquainted with him, she realized that he was caring as well. Mr. Harper wanted Kate and her classmates to do their best and learn as much as possible. He offered to give Kate extra help after class a few times a week and was very patient with her.

Now, on the evening of the spelling bee, Kate was nervous. At the same time, she was happy and very excited. She knew her mom and Mr. Harper were proud of her. Kate was also proud of herself for having refused to let dyslexia get in the way of her goals.

Kate was brought onto the auditorium's stage with the other contestants. Together they were introduced to the audience. Kate noticed her mom sitting in the front row. Mr. Harper was sitting to her left. Kate was pleased to see them. She knew they would bring her good luck!

The principal, Mrs. Curtis, explained the spelling bee's procedures. Then she called upon a student to spell a word. The spelling bee had begun!

Kate listened carefully. She tried spelling the words in her head, but the letters came out all scrambled.

Suddenly it was Kate's turn! Mrs. Curtis asked her to spell "pneumonia."

Kate hesitated. But then she looked down into the front row. Mr. Harper was smiling at her. He knew that Kate could spell that word! Mr. Harper once had Kate read a story in class about a girl who was sick with pneumonia.

Kate took a deep breath, picturing the word in her head. "Pneumonia," she said. "P-n-e-u-m-o-n-i-a. Pneumonia."

"That's right," said Mrs. Curtis.

Kate was thrilled. She had gotten her first word right!

Even with the great start that she had gotten off to, Kate knew that it would be difficult to win the spelling bee. She also knew that she would have to battle dyslexia for the rest of her life. Still, she had found a love of reading that she could take with her wherever she might go.

Dedicated Teachers

Have you had teachers like Mrs. Miller, Miss Zahn, and Mr. Harper?

Mr. Harper helps Kate by encouraging her to never give up. He keeps her focused during class by not letting her talk. He also helps her after class, and shows her great support at the spelling bee.

Teachers everywhere work hard to make sure their students learn all they need to know. It may seem that they expect too much sometimes, but your teachers care about you and your classmates and are dedicated in helping you to do your best.

Can you think of a teacher who has acted this way? If you can, then you are fortunate to have been in that teacher's class!